Marin Headlands

Portals of Time

by

Harold and Ann Lawrence Gilliam

Contents

The Golden Gate National Park Association is a non-
profit membership organization established to support
the education, conservation and research programs of
the Golden Gate National Recreation Area.

PUBLISHED BY THE
GOLDEN GATE NATIONAL
PARK ASSOCIATION

ISBN 1-883869-13-7

First-time visitors to the Bay Area
are often amazed at the sight of open hills directly across the Golden
Gate from the highrise towers and densely populated neighborhoods
of San Francisco. Rising abruptly from the swiftly flowing waters of
the strait to a height of nearly 1,000 feet above sea level, the southern
edge of Marin County makes an eloquent statement about the relation
of a metropolis to the natural world.

The Marin Headlands, part of the Golden Gate National
Recreation Area, consists of 15 square miles of beaches, cliffs, valleys
and ridges inhabited by very few humans and a very large population
of wild animals. This unique juxtaposition of San Francisco's crowded
urban setting and the open space of a spectacular landscape offers an
opportunity seldom given to city dwellers—a view not only into space
but into time, with tangible evidence of the ages that have passed and
intimations of those to come.

The ocean, which shaped these headlands, was the first
geological feature on Earth and the source of the life that eventually
spread across the continents. The marine creatures swimming offshore
here represent our own "ancestors;" the rocks visible in the cliffs are
remnants of old sea beds formed when all of California was under
water. The cliffs themselves have been carved as the mountains rose out
of the ocean and as sea level advanced at the end of the last Ice Age—
an ongoing process that continues to shape this edge of the continent.

It was in lagoons such as those in the Headlands that life slowly emerged from the waters to the land—first the sea plants that could grow in brackish water and evolved to survive on the shores, then amphibious animals that developed into land dwellers.

During the course of this evolution, plant and animal life spread from the lagoons and ponds and streams to the riparian zones along the shores, the meadows, and the hillsides, developing over the eons into the many forms we encounter there today. Back in the ocean are seals and sea lions and whales—mammals that evolved on land and returned to the sea.

Perhaps as residents of the cities around the Bay, we are metaphorically undergoing a parallel return of our own—in a faster time frame. Our species first lived in the wilds, then became urban dwellers and are now returning as visitors to the natural scenes from which we came. As we begin to spend more time in nature and to understand its workings, we are perhaps "evolving" into creatures who will adapt our ways of living and working to the needs and processes of the natural environment, the Earth itself. In this sense the close encounter of the urban with the natural here in the Headlands can offer a view of the future as well as the past, a new perspective through these portals of time.

How the Park Came About

In the 1940s, Dr. Edgar Wayburn, a San Francisco physician and volunteer Sierra Club leader, looked across the Golden Gate from his San Francisco home and envisioned preserving the open hills of Marin County as a permanent park for future generations. In the 1960s he founded People for a Golden Gate National Recreation Area, mobilized public opinion, and enlisted the powerful energies of Representative Phillip Burton, who put through the legislation that created the Golden Gate National Recreation Area in 1972.

§

Cliffs and Beaches

THE GOLDEN GATE WAS A SHOCKER. Eighteenth- and nineteenth-
century explorers were astounded by the spectacle of this cliff-bound
strait where San Francisco Bay opens to the Pacific. Padre Pedro Font
in 1776 called it "a prodigy of Nature," and John C. Fremont in 1846,
inspired by its fancied resemblance to the Golden Horn of ancient
Byzantium, the crossroads between Europe and Asia, named it
"Chrysopylae" or "Golden Gate," as the potential portal to the coming
era of the Pacific.

Similarly, the first scientists investigating the geology of the
Marin Headlands were fascinated and awed by what they saw, and
were unable to explain the fantastic rock formations revealed in the
wave-cut cliffs along the shore of the strait. It was not until the late
1970s that the new plate-tectonics theory—describing the motion of
plates of the Earth's crust—enabled geologists to begin to piece
together the extraordinary story of what they called the Marin
Headlands block. That block, they say, evidently originated thousands
of miles away in the depths of the equatorial Pacific, made the journey
here over a period of 100 million years, and continues to be shaped by
interactions between the ocean and the continent's edge.

As you explore these rocks in the Headlands—particularly in
the cliffs at Rodeo Cove, Bonita Cove, and Tennessee Cove, but also in
upland road cuts and outcrops—you are peering into eons of the Earth's
history and seeing the results of some of the planetary processes that
shaped the seas and continents. With a good hand-lens you can also
look into biologic time and see fossils of some early forms of life, single-
celled organisms called "radiolarians." The reddish rock in which the
fossils appear is radiolarian chert. Chert originally formed in level layers
on the floor of the Pacific, one to five inches thick, but later contorted
so they now resemble not so much crumpled pages in a book (as some
of the early scientists noted) as intricate sculpturings by some artists in
abstract designs—arches, domes, chevrons, and parabolas in innumerable variations of form and texture.

Along with the chert you can see two other main types of rock in the Headlands Block: basalt and sandstone. The basalt is often dark green (its alternate name is "greenstone"), but it weathers to reddish brown or orange. It appears not in contorted layers like the chert but often in pillow shapes, hence the name "pillow basalt." Alternately with the chert and basalt in these cliffs and outcrops are large masses of sandstone, most often dark gray, weathering to light brown and buff.

Only the hardiest of plants find a toe-hold in the multi-layered chert cliffs of the Headlands.

The Long Snowfall

How the Marin Headlands Block was born in the far Pacific and arrived here after its 100-million-year journey is a mind-boggling story involving the basic processes of the planet's surface. As described by plate-tectonics theory, from giant fissures in the ocean floor—some thousands of miles long—molten lava intermittently flowed up like a fountain from the Earth's hot interior about 200 million years ago (as it continues to do today). When the lava encountered the cold sea water, it congealed into bulb-shaped masses, forming stone pillows about a yard long, convex on top, with the concave bottom neatly fitting the top of the lower pillow.

While these rocks were being formed as pillow basalt on the old ocean floor, high above in the surface waters the sunlight generated multitudes of single-celled micro-organisms with shells of lime or silica. As they died, their shells slowly sank toward the basaltic bottom over millions of years in what Rachel Carson in *The Sea Around Us* called "the long snowfall." The lime shells gradually dissolved, but the silica shells remained and accumulated on the ocean floor, along with reddish dust that had blown into the ocean from some far-off continental deserts, much as the sands of the Sahara still blow out into the Atlantic. Eventually the shells and the dust solidified into the rock we see now.

The newly forming ocean floor—basalt topped with chert—sporadically spread outward from the crustal fountains and formed the colossal plates that "float" on the molten magma of the Earth's mantle. As the oceanic plate moved thousands of miles from the spreading zone toward the North American continent, the continent itself was moving westward, propelled by a similar spreading zone in the Atlantic.

When the moving ocean floor approached the continent, sand that had eroded from the land was washed into the sea and solidified into the sandstone that you now see in the cliffs. As the plates moved together over a period of several more millions of years, the heavier ocean floor slid under the leading edge of the lighter continental plate. In the geologists' term it was "subducted." But during this long slow subduction, some of the downward-plunging ocean floor, including what is now the Marin Headlands Block, was scraped off by the leading edge of the continental plate and contorted into the tortuous forms we now see in the cliffs and roadcuts, particularly the chert layers.

The Drowning of the Dunes

To the south, the Headlands Block has been sheared by an unknown fault that lies somewhere at the bottom of the Golden Gate—a fracture that may be responsible for the creation of the strait itself; the rocks crushed along the fault could have been worn down by erosion. The same rocks that you see in the Marin Headlands Block appear south of the Gate in the highest hills of San Francisco: Twin Peaks, Mount Sutro, and Mount Davidson, where the same kind of contorted chert is readily visible in the road cuts and outcrops.

If these multimillion-year views into time begin to stagger the imagination, consider some more recent events that have shaped parts of the Headlands, particularly the beaches. If you had been on these hills during the peak of the last Ice Age, a mere 20,000 years ago, you would have looked west not to the ocean but to a nearly barren landscape of dunes. Because part of the Earth's water supply was frozen into the great ice sheets, sea level at that time was several hundred feet lower than at present. The shoreline here was behind the granite peaks now known as the Farallon Islands, 20 miles to the west.

The dune sand was derived mainly from the Sierra Nevada and brought down by rivers cutting their way through the rising Coast Ranges to the ocean. As the Earth's climate grew warmer and the ice sheets began to melt, their waters drained to the oceans, and sea level rose all over the planet. The dunes were gradually submerged, although some remains of them, carried by the wind up against the foot of the Headlands, are still visible on the slopes above the southwest corner of Rodeo Lagoon.

THE RISING OCEAN FLOODED the river-cut gorge that is now the Golden Gate and transformed an inland valley into the present San Francisco Bay. At the same time it flooded smaller coastal indentations, such as the valley now occupied by Rodeo Lagoon. In a few thousand years the waves, battering the Headlands, have carved these cliffs and distributed the resulting sand and gravel along the shoreline, forming at Rodeo Cove a barrier beach that dammed off the drowned valley. As you walk now on Rodeo Beach, the coarse sand and pebbles beneath your feet are reddish in color, derived from the kind of red chert you can see in the cliffs, mixed with gray and brown fragments of sandstone and basalt. Green pebbles that look like jade are pieces of green chert, and occasionally you may see, among the pebbles, orange-colored carnelians (some of them veined with white quartz) which were once part of the basalt in the cliffs. But the dominant reddish sand and gravel have been eroded from the chert formations, both in the nearby seacliffs and in upland outcrops. Owing to the durability of that very hard rock, this beach is one of the few places in the world with sand grains of such large size.

Rodeo Beach sand and gravel

Monument of Pillows

Midway along the beach at Bonita Cove, about a mile northeast of the Point Bonita Lighthouse, stands another monument to the antiquity of the Earth, a pinnacle rising from a wave-cut platform to a height of about 30 feet above sea level. You don't have to look very hard to see the "pillows" of rock that mark this as pillow basalt; they appear as semi-detached boulders protruding from the monument wall. Some of them are green with tints of red; some are dark gray to greenish. Pillows of the same kind are even now sporadically being created in the depths of the ocean, wherever fissures in the Earth's crust emit molten lavas. This monument reveals some of the best examples of pillow basalt to be found anywhere on Earth—comparable to those in the depths of the ocean.

Along the beach east of the monument, you'll find greenish basalt boulders tinted with colorful pinkish-to-purple limestone, veined in some places with quartz—colors that become luminescent when the rock is wet with spray from the surf. Walking toward the east end of the cove, you can see gray sandstone embedded with angular fragments of chert. In the cliffs at the east end of the beach is a dramatic contact zone where sandstone was deposited on top of the chert before both strata were up-ended.

You can get another good view into geologic time at Kirby Cove, where you walk through groves of eucalyptus, Monterey pine and Monterey cypress (planted by the Army) and cross a man-made dune to the beach and a superb view of the nearby Golden Gate Bridge. On the point at the east end of the beach, toward the Bridge, are two sets of chert beds folded first in one direction and then another, forming convoluted patterns.

Kirby Cove

Color in the Cove

Some of the most eloquently sculptured seacliffs in the Headlands are at Tennessee Cove. The high sheer wall on the north side of the cove is primarily chert, hollowed by millennial waves into shallow caverns under layered arches that are greenish on the surface, except near the cornerstone of the wall where the contorted layers are yellow-gold. Some 75 feet up the cliff is a "keyhole"—a ten-foot clerestory window in the wall affording a view of the sky. It is a result of waves from both sides of the wall cutting into a fault zone and undermining the wall until it broke through at its narrowest point, creating the window.

The wall at the south end of the cove is even more spectacular; here the basalt has been exposed by the waves beneath the overlying chert, which here is not only reddish but warm gold to orange. In the coves to the south, you perhaps reach the climax of the Headlands rock displays—red and gold chert layers, outcrops of pillow basalt, high masses of gray sandstone, and landslides combining all these rock types below colorful and intricate mural sculptures that intrigue the imagination. But here or whenever you're near the water, keep an eye on the waves and watch out for incoming tides.

The Coming of Life

Between the fossil radiolarians in the chert of these cliffs and the teeming life you see now along these shores are 200 million years of evolution. Some of the oldest forms of life living here now—unrelated to the radiolarians—are the kelps and the jellyfish-type organisms washed up on the shoreline, followed by the barnacles, mussels, limpets, sea urchins and starfish you can find on the rocks at low tide. Later came the free-swimming fishes, ancestors of surf perch, sea bass, and salmon, some of them here in schools whose presence is indicated by excited flights of sea birds offshore.

The first primitive birds, unlike any here now, began to evolve from reptiles beginning 150 million years ago, when the radiolarians you can see now in the rocks were accumulating on the sea floor. The earliest of the birds developed much later. First came those expert swimmers and divers, the grebes, black-and-white or gray-and-white duck-like birds that fly in an ungainly fashion with drooping necks. Next in line of evolution came the pelicans, whose 6-1/2 foot wingspread makes them majestic in flight.

Among other primitive birds you might see here are the cormorants, large black birds flying low over the water, long necks extended, or perched upright on posts, spreading their wings to dry.

Later in the order of evolution came the big herons and egrets, the ducks, geese, turkey vultures, hawks, sandpipers, gulls, owls, hummingbirds, jays, thrushes, and blackbirds.

Snowy egret

Although there were small, insignificant mammals during the latter part of the age of reptiles 65 to 135 million years ago, the higher mammals did not appear until the reptiles were no longer dominant. Some of them evolved on land and returned to the sea: you may glimpse the head of a seal or sea lion riding the swells offshore. Or you might spot the far-off spout of a California gray whale en route in the fall from the seas off the Aleutians to the warm lagoons of southern Baja California, where they mate and give birth.

THE MOST RECENT EVOLUTIONARY arrival visible here was the two-legged mammal that you can see exploring this shore or lying on the sand when the weather permits. Humans are only the latest of the forms of life that can be traced back 200 million years to the time of the radiolarians in these cliffs—and far beyond. Observing here in the Headlands the various stages in the evolution of the Earth and its life forms, we may wonder what unpredictable shapes of land and life the next 200 million years will bring.

The Point Bonita Light Station

By the early 1850s, it was evident that a lighthouse was needed at the Golden Gate. Ship traffic was already heavy and the hazards of the strong tides that moved through the Gate were compounded by summer fog and winter storms.

The Lighthouse Board, later called the Lighthouse Service, chose Point Bonita on the north shore of the Golden Gate for the location because a light there would be visible in all directions. In 1853, Congress appropriated $25,000 for construction. Of this amount, $7,000 was used to buy one of the finest lens available, a Fresnel lens that was made in Paris and shipped around Cape Horn.

The lighthouse, its beacon proudly ornamented with iron gargoyles in the shape of American eagles, went into operation in May, 1855. There were soon complaints, however, because the lighthouse had been built atop a high ridge nearly 300 feet above the water and thick fog frequently blotted out the light beam. It was decided to build a new lighthouse station at the tip of Point Bonita, called Land's End, where there would be less fog. A building housing a louder fog signal would be built close by.

Land's End was a particularly difficult site for a major light station. Point Bonita is known for its high cliffs and unstable rock formations, and construction was frequently halted by landslides.

Nevertheless, work slowly progressed, even though the workmen confronted life-threatening situations almost every day. In Guardians of the Golden Gate, *historians Ralph and Lisa Shanks relate that at one point the men constructing the trail to Land's End* "had to cross a 100-foot deep chasm on a single unsupported board using only a rope to hang onto."

Point Bonita Life-Saving Station crew in their 18-foot lifeboat.

The trail was finished. A landing platform was built at Bonita Cove and connected to the trail above by a railroad and staircase. The fog signal building was constructed. For the foundation of the lighthouse, a rectangular three-room structure was built of heavy masonry on the levelled rock at Land's End. On this foundation was placed the upper half of the original lighthouse—polygonal watch room, lantern room, gargoyles and all. On February 2, 1877, the Point Bonita light was relighted at its present location.

The lighthouse keepers at Point Bonita and their families belonged to a heroic tradition of public service. Ill-paid and ill-housed in the early years, they dedicated their lives to keeping the light going and the fog signal operating. Norma Engels remembers in her memoir, Three Beams of Light, *that her father, an assistant lighthouse keeper, was on duty during the 1906 earthquake. Despite his terrible fears for his family, he stuck to his post.*

In 1898, when the Point Bonita Life-Saving Station was established, another group of courageous men and their families joined the lighthouse community. The "surfmen"—as they were called—had to be ready to man their 18-foot cars at any time and row out to rescue the ship-wrecked and near shipwrecked. The surfmen's motto was ominous: "You have to go out, but you don't have to come in." In the 1940s, long after power boats had been intro-duced, the Life-Saving Station at Point Bonita was disbanded.

The Point Bonita Light Station has never stopped evolving. Around 1900, a new fog signal building—of harmonious design—was built in front of the lighthouse. Several decades later, the traditional fixed light was changed to a light that flashes a distinctive signal. The fog signal, which has seen many musical and not-so-musical changes, has been converted to an electronic signal.

The biggest change of all came in 1981 when the light station was automated and the process of transfer-ring it to the National Park Service was begun. The lantern room and the fog signal building remain under the control of the Coast Guard.

Whatever the changes, the Point Bonita Lighthouse has remained its classic self, shining its light into the dark-ness through the same Fresnel lens that came around the Horn in 1855.

§

Lagoons and Ponds

AS YOU COME DOWN INTO RODEO VALLEY, one of the features that strikes your eye is the sky-silvered surface of a lagoon lying between hills that are green in spring, straw-colored in summer. Nearly a mile long and five hundred feet wide, Rodeo Lagoon is the largest of the lagoons and ponds in the Marin Headlands. Like the others, it swells in size when it receives the runoff from the winter rains. The lagoon is basically fresh, but slightly brackish, owing to saltier water from the waves that occasionally breach the barrier dunes. Consequently, it provides a perfect habitat for the endangered inch-long fish known as the tidewater goby, which can breed only in water of low salinity. A much smaller lagoon, also brackish, lies over the hills to the north at the mouth of Tennessee Creek.

Engineered Ponds

While the lagoons, though strongly affected by human activities, can be considered natural features, the handful of freshwater ponds scattered along Tennessee and Rodeo creeks are not. They were all created by dams built at various times by ranchers and the Army. Yet these engineered ponds have evolved into closely knit communities of plants and animals that play an integral place in the natural world of the Headlands.

The freshwater ponds and their marshy edges abound with plants and animals. For a first-hand look, explore the two ponds along Rodeo Creek just below the Visitor Center. In spring and summer, these ponds are almost unapproachable except where picnic areas have been carved out of the dense surrounding growth. Here picnickers find themselves virtually hidden in a small forest of alders and arroyo willows, sedges and grasses and numerous other plants.

The standard bearer of the marshy plants is the common cattail, which grows abundantly in both fresh- and saltwater marshes. Its brown spike, sausage-shaped or cigar-shaped, depending on your point of view, inspires among most people a friendly recognition. Coast Miwoks and other Native Americans found many uses for this plant.

Blue darner dragonfly

The fluff that it produces to parachute its seeds was used by mothers for what we would call disposable diapers. The pollen was used to make a tasty bread, while the rhizome was roasted or sometimes dried and ground into meal. The leaves were woven into floor mats and used to thatch roofs.

Cattails and the tules, sedges, and grasses that accompany them have a paramount importance for bird life. They offer hidden recesses for nesting and harbor larvae that are an important source of protein for young birds when they hatch. The marshy plant life also serves as a habitat for crayfish, muskrats, frogs, and water snakes upon which larger birds and animals prey. This is the domain of the great blue heron that stands or wades slowly and deliberately through the shallows and then, with a sudden thrust of its long thin neck and arrow-sharp beak, seizes a frog or fish.

The First Fliers

On the edge of a pond on a spring day, a thousand presences of creatures seen and unseen are felt. In the water, murky with sediment, live all kinds of unfamiliar beings, some of which when seen in close-up photographs seem designed by a demonic Walt Disney. One of these fearsome-looking creatures is the voracious dragonfly nymph that will metamorphose into the equally voracious four-winged dragonfly. Dragonflies most commonly found at the Marin Headlands are the green darners and the blue darners. All insects seem to evoke the unfathomable past; but the dragonfly more than most, for it is heir to the great dragonfly-like creatures, some with a wingspread of 30 inches, that flew in the sunlight and shadow of the coal forests of the Carboniferous Age. Dragonflies and others of their insect kin were the first creatures to fly. It was another 50 million years before the flying reptiles ancestral to birds began their first tentative flights.

The dragonfly nymph lives its entire feeding and growing stage under water in freshwater ponds. Concealed by its coloring, the nymph lies in wait for its prey, which it grabs using a formidable weapon—an extendable lower lip set with teeth. The prey include larvae, aquatic insects, tadpoles, and even small fish larger than the nymph itself. Reaching maturity after two or three years, the nymph crawls out of the water and molts for the last time. Its wings are released, and after a period of drying them in the sun, the dragonfly takes off. Its antique past remains close to it, for unlike more recently evolved winged insects it cannot fold its wings at rest, but must leave them flat. Extraordinarily able flyers, dragonflies attain speeds of 20 miles an hour or more and can easily chase down other winged insects which they locate by means of their enormous bulging eyes.

Walkers on the Water

It is in the shallows that pond life is most abundant. Here, as naturalist Peter Farb observes, there is a "just-right balance of water temperature, sunlight, oxygen in solution, food and living space." Hordes of tadpoles rush this way and that, demonstrating the blind generosity of creation. Backswimmers and water boatmen, small beetle-like insects, propel themselves along using their enlarged back legs—the backswimmer on its back and the water boatman right side up. Caddis-fly and mosquito larvae, nymphs of dragonflies and damselflies thrive.

Plankton grows easily in the pond shallows, providing food for the tiny crustaceans and protozoa, which are eaten by such small predators as the backswimmers that are in turn eaten by the nymphs, fish, and other carnivorous creatures. And so on up the food chain. It is this abundance of small-scaled life that supports the pond turtles and frogs and the larger life of the pond.

But the life of the pond also includes the surface, for owing to the intense attraction that water molecules have for one another, the surface film of the water is unexpectedly strong and elastic. Here lives another familiar insect, that champion skater, the water strider that glides ably along on the surface film supported by skinny, thread-like legs. The water striders' legs are well designed for its niche in the natural world. The claw is placed far enough back from the tip of its leg so as not to break the surface film, and the tip itself is covered with tiny hairs that repel the water. In the shadows that play about the bottoms of ponds and streams, it seems as if the insect wears wide flat boots resembling those of Charlie Chaplin, but these are just shadows of indentations caused by the weight of the insect. Water striders prey on smaller insects that have fallen onto the surface film and locate them by the ripple patterns they make as they struggle.

California newt

Birds of Winter

It is birds, however, that give the lagoons and ponds—and beaches, too—their larger dimension. Insects were the first creatures to achieve flight, but, with the exception of butterflies and moths, flying insects, no matter how adept, have never aroused the human imagination. Birds have. In almost every culture birds are symbols of the human spirit and its winged search for truth.

Bird watching is best in fall and winter at the Marin Headlands. Picture the scene on a winter day at Rodeo Beach, when the tide is receding. Flocks of sparrow-sized least sandpipers run back and forth, picking up small fly larvae, crustaceans, and worms from the wet surface left by the waves. Their tiny legs move so fast that they seem to be skating, not running. They are joined by large flocks of western sandpipers, the most common shorebird in the Bay Area during the winter months. Slightly bigger than the least sandpipers, western sandpipers boldly wade belly-deep into the edges of the retreating surf, briskly searching out worms, crustaceans and such tiny mollusks as gem clams. A few feet away, ten or twelve sanderlings in their pale winter plumage, bills partly open, probe the wet sand for similar tasty morsels. Well aware of the rhythms of the ocean, the birds scoot nimbly up on the beach as the next wall of foam comes tumbling in. The tide is out now, but as it rises, the shorebirds will retreat inland, some to the safety of the sandy beach at the western end of

Peregrine falcon

Rodeo Lagoon, others to mudflats along the coast or San Francisco Bay.

Above, a predator appears, a merlin or possibly a peregrine falcon. The small shorebirds shoot into the air, each kind wheeling in unison this way and that, the sanderlings flashing luminous white wing stripes, the western sandpipers revealing white underparts as surprising as sudden snow. A few grayish-brown willets, larger shorebirds of undistinguished hue, have been probing nearby for marine invertebrates. They also start off in alarm, revealing wings unexpectedly striped with broad bands of white and black. As they fly, they utter their eerie unforgettable cry, one that well expresses the uncertainties of life on the shoreline.

Farther north on the beach some ring-billed gulls, named for the black circle around their yellow bills, pay no attention to the shorebirds that alight and once again probe for food. Offshore, ably riding the waves, are four or five surf scoters, small black sea ducks that dive zestfully and always come up in some unexpected place. Perched on Bird Rock at the south end of the beach, a pelagic cormorant stands spread-eagled, revealing the white rump patches of its breeding plumage.

The sandpipers and willets may be joined at one time or another by other shorebirds, including large brown and buff marbled godwits, long-billed curlews, and greater yellow-legs. Not all of these birds, particularly the larger ones, come every year to the Marin Headlands. Some may be found one year and some the next. They and other shorebirds do not compete with each other for food. The food resources of beach and mudflats are neatly partitioned among them according to their size and to the shape of their bills and behavior patterns.

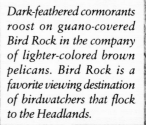

Dark-feathered cormorants roost on guano-covered Bird Rock in the company of lighter-colored brown pelicans. Bird Rock is a favorite viewing destination of birdwatchers that flock to the Headlands.

The Marin Headlands Visitor Center in Fort Barry
Chapel greets visitors with information about hiking and
camping, interpretive walks, natural history exhibits and
a bookstore. Nearby, a mallard raises its family in the
shelter of the lagoon.

Divers and Dabblers

The Marin Headlands is on the Pacific Flyway, one of four general north-south routes taken by migrating birds across the United States. Numbers of migrating waterfowl returning south in fall stop to rest at Rodeo Lagoon, and many decide to stay for the winter.

At Rodeo Lagoon on a winter day, red-breasted mergansers, the males black crested, float jauntily on the rippling surface, occasionally diving for fish that they seize with long red spike-like bills. Flocks of canvasback ducks are also enjoying the Lagoon's largesse. They dive for plants growing on the bottom, often returning—as naturalist Allen Fish notes—with muddy faces. A flock of buffleheads, miniature diving ducks, bob up and down on the water; one bufflehead serves as sentry while the others dive. Wigeons, which are dabblers, not divers, go bottoms up, submerging their heads and necks while feeding on the plant life near the water's surface. Dabbling ducks and diving ducks manage their "take offs" in different ways. Dabblers spring directly into the air; divers patter or taxi along the surface of the water before becoming fully airborne.

Later, seen from the Visitor Center in the afternoon light, the buffleheads and canvasbacks and other light-colored ducks twinkle against the dark water as the sun engages their white parts. In another few months, many of these waterfowl and many of the shorebirds will be far north of here on their annual migrations to their nesting grounds in Alaska and Canada. Curiously, some of the longest treks are those made by the tiny sanderlings that breed on the islands off the Arctic, and by the equally small western and least sandpipers that breed along the Alaskan coast.

Nesting Time

When spring comes, the birds living year-round at the lagoons and ponds begin their nesting, mostly near the freshwater ponds. Among them are the small brown pied-billed grebes, the most solitary of all the North American grebes, which artfully construct raft-like nests well hidden in the reeds of the freshwater ponds. Another nester beside the freshwater ponds is the shy long-billed marsh wren, located more easily by its flute-like song than by sight. Each year mating pairs of these clever birds build two to five nests on the ground near freshwater ponds. Only one is to be used; the others are decoys. Small black coots also prefer freshwater ponds for nesting. Noisy, scrappy birds, they have a remarkable repertoire of fourteen displays—expressing alarm, distress, aggression, etc.,—that doubtless play a part in the parents' efforts to safeguard the nestlings.

Killdeer

Killdeers, brown and white birds easily identified by their two black neck bands and unmistakable call ("kil-deeah"), lay their eggs on the gravelly surfaces near Rodeo Lagoon, a background that provides almost perfect camouflage. If a raccoon or other predator appears, the adult feigns a broken wing and awkwardly flutters away from the chicks, luring the predator away with the tease of an easy meal.

The Quiet Seasons

The beaches and lagoons are quiet in spring, although there are some new arrivals in May or June. Among them are the dark red-billed Heermann's gulls up from their nesting sites on the islands off Baja California. They are among the seven or eight kinds of gulls that confidently ride the air currents over the Marin Headlands. The large western gulls, recognizable by their dark backs and wings, white underparts and pink feet, nest at Point Bonita and are year-round dwellers. California gulls—gray mantled, black wing tips spotted with white—are common in every season but summer, when they nest at Mono Lake. The red spot on their bills, evident at close range, is the target at which the young chicks peck in order to get the parent to regurgitate food for them. California and western gulls often stand on various perches at Rodeo Lagoon, some-times on one leg, a posture whose purpose is to conserve body heat.

The intensity of bird life at Rodeo Lagoon and the ponds continues to diminish as spring slides into summer. Then, as summer is passing into fall, the shorebirds return from their brief nesting season in the far north. Later in fall, the migrating ducks and geese stop off at the lagoon on their long flights south, and some decide to stay the winter. The cycle starts again.

Artists of the Updraft

Of all the birds that inhabit the beaches and lagoons of the Headlands, perhaps the most impressive is a species whose seasonal presence provides a sense of ancient time and decorum. Few other birds have as long a lineage in the scale of evolution. These prototypes of avian antiquity are the brown pelicans that begin arriving in May or June from their nesting grounds on the islands off southern Baja California.

These dignified birds feed on small fish that swim near the surface and catch them by executing spectacular aerial dives of twenty or thirty feet which end in great splashes. They use their large gular pouches as fishnets on the dive, emptying the water out when they come to the surface and swallowing the fish. That is, if they can, for they are often followed by piratical gulls that try to seize the hard-earned meal. Brown pelicans are consummately skillful flyers, artists of the updraft, sedately cruising above the beach and ocean, descending to take advantage of the updraft of waves to skim their crests or even glide in the troughs between them. At Rodeo Lagoon they float affably with their avian companions.

Since DDT was banned in the United States in 1972, the brown pelican population, decimated by the pesticide, has made a comeback. Some authorities believe, however, that the danger is not over for the pelicans and other migratory birds, as DDT still lingers in the food chain and is used in countries where the birds winter. Human activities continue to have damaging impacts on the ecosystems of the planet, and birds are sometimes the most vulnerable victims. Actions that jeopardize their survival may also jeopardize our own.

LEAVING THE MARIN HEADLANDS, perhaps turning for a last glimpse of Rodeo Lagoon and the ocean beyond, we may reflect on the thought that many religious traditions have held the earth to be sacred. Upon us has been laid the responsibility of stewardship.

The Vaqueros

For most of the first half of the nineteenth century, the windy slopes and valleys of the Marin Headlands were the domain of vaqueros tending herds of the half-wild sharp-horned cattle found on early California ranchos. During these years, the Headlands belonged first to Mission San Rafael, and later formed part of an 18,000-acre ranch owned by the English-born entrepreneur William Richardson.

The vaqueros, who had come north from Mexico, used techniques of herding cattle that had been brought over from Spain. But not all the vaqueros were Mexican. Many were Native Americans, probably Ohlones (Costanoans) and Coast Miwoks. Using only a simple blanket as a saddle, the Native American vaqueros equalled the Mexican vaqueros as cattle herders and were in charge of rounding up the cattle twice a year for slaughter for hides and tallow, the chief products of the ranchos.

For the Marin Headlands, the era of the vaqueros ended in 1856 when financial difficulties forced William Richardson to sell Rancho Sausalito to San Francisco financier Samuel Throckmorton. But the era left a remembrance in the changed landscape of the Headlands.

Wild oats and other European annual grasses were introduced by seeds that crossed the Atlantic in the hides of Spanish cattle and swiftly displaced the native bunchgrass.

The vaqueros' dress, which included flat-brimmed felt hats and short jackets, was Mexican with a Spanish touch. From the vaqueros' traditions came that quintessential American hero, the western cowboy.

Weather

The eons-old war between the sea and the continent is waged in regular cycles in the Headlands, when the Pacific sends its foggy aerial armadas landward until the continental forces drive back the sea vapors with warm dry air from the inland valleys. The conflict is readily visible in spring, summer, and early fall. The prevailing northwest winds push the ocean currents down the coast, causing frigid water from the sunless depths to rise to the surface, chill the sea air, and condense the air vapor into the great fog bank that intermittently blankets the coast and the offshore waters.

Portuguese dairy ranch scene from the early 20th century.

The Dairy Ranchers

By the 1880s, Tennessee Valley and other parts of the Marin Headlands had been subdivided into small dairy ranches operated by Portuguese families from the Azores. Their lives were hard, but they undertook their never-ending work with vigor and courage. Their day centered around the milkings at 4 a.m. and 4 p.m. Between milkings came the tasks of cleaning the milk equipment and barn and feeding and caring for 80 to 90 cattle.

Tennessee Valley was not the best place for dairy ranching. Frequent summer fog made it difficult to dry hay grown on the ranches and the dairymen had to buy hay as well as feed for the cows. Water shortages in summer were also troublesome.

Dairy ranching made for an isolated life. Children went daily to school in Mill Valley, but the adults seldom left the ranch except to go to Sunday mass in Mill Valley or Sausalito. Family ties were close, however, and there was a peacefulness to the life that all remembered.

The families cherished their Portuguese heritage. Each year on Pentecost, they joined other Portuguese families in celebrating the Holy Ghost Festa, a religious festival particularly important in the Azores. On this occasion a "queen" was crowned, grand parades were held on the main street in Sausalito, offerings were given to the poor, and all sat down to a meal of the traditional sopa and bread. "Chamarittas," which resembled American square dances, followed.

By the 1960s, this way of life had come to an end at the Marin Headlands. There was little money to be made in dairy ranching and most of the ranchers had sold their land.

§

Woodlands

IN THE MARIN HEADLANDS as elsewhere, life is most abundant in
the presence of water. As if drawn by the memory of its evolutionary
origins in the ocean, its emergence from the seas to the lagoons and
marshes, its ventures up rivers and streams to habitats on their banks,
life clusters along shorelines and watercourses. Just as humans tend to
build their communities on bodies of water, plants and animals are
most abundant wherever water accumulates in the course of the hydro-
logic cycle. They proliferate in areas of heaviest rainfall (hence the
super abundance of life in the tropical rainforests), on shorelines, in
and around lakes and ponds and streams.

There are two principal watercourses in the Headlands, one
each in the two principal east-west valleys—Rodeo and Tennessee.
It is along these small creeks that the woodlands are most prolific. The
riparian zone along the streams is an interacting community of plant
and animal life and moving water. Vegetation along the banks changes
the light and temperature of the water, protects the banks from erosion, buffers rain runoff, catches sediment, provides shelter for fishes
and camouflage for reptiles, insects, birds and mammals.

As you walk the trails of the Headlands, you'll note very soon
that most of the creeks are marked by bowers of that prolific tree
eulogized in song and story, the willow. In most places the willows are
overgrown shrubs, forming almost impenetrable thickets along and
over the creeks; in some places they may grow to trees up to 30 feet
high. You will recognize the willows by their yellow-ridged bark and
their long, narrow gray-green leaves that turn orange-yellow in the fall
before they drop, leaving bare limbs. The leaves are sometimes marked
by a bright red spot, the willow-leaf gall. The gall is not part of the leaf
but is produced by a wasp that emits a chemical causing the gall to
form as a protective "cocoon" for its eggs. The willow-leaf gall is just
one of many kinds of galls deposited by many kinds of insects. Some of
them grow on the tree's twigs and look like inch-long pine cones.

Coast Miwok Indians made ingenious use of the willows.
The twigs were valuable for weaving baskets and fish nets, and the
larger branches were used in building their kochas—thatched houses.
The bark was the source of red and brown dyes for the baskets and

also was useful as a medicinal tea; it contains salicylic acid, the same pain-relieving chemical found in aspirin. The inner bark was made into rope, and large stems were used to make whistles and clappers and to lift rocks heated by campfires.

Mixed in with the willows in the streamside thickets you may find alders, blackberries, and ferns, particularly bracken. Animals find the leaves make succulent meals, and the thickets are perfect hiding places for nests and for giving birth to young. Other common riparian plants among the willows resemble those you see on the banks of the lagoons and ponds: cattails, horsetails, and yellow mimulus or monkey-flower. You'll also see, in the pools and banks of the creeks, some of the animals that frequent the ponds: those adaptable amphibians that represent the emergence of life from water to land—salamanders, newts, and frogs. Their dry-land counterparts, representing later stages of evolution, are lizards and toads. Also appearing occasionally in the streamside woodlands are dry-land mammals that come for a drink—deer, raccoons, bobcats, and foxes.

Among the birds you may see around the creek banks, looking for water and insects, are sparrows, blackbirds, and towhees. Perhaps the most conspicuous is the male red-winged blackbird, which often perches on top of a reed or willow, spreads his tail, droops his wings, raises his crimson epaulets and emits a musical twanging call that indicates this is his territory and no competitors are welcome. Other male redwings trespassing in search of food will cover their epaulets to be more inconspicuous. Should the owner of the territory spot them and give chase, they quickly leave, in *de facto* recognition of the owner's property rights.

Butterflies

Mission blue butterfly

On a spring day in the Headlands, the butterflies are in full "bloom." On the Bobcat Trail among the masses of yellow mustard you may find several varieties, including cabbage whites and orange sulphurs; and around the lupine and fennel the orange-spotted pipevine swallowtails and Anna's swallowtails. Blue varieties frequent the Coastal Trail where they are joined by Sara orange tips, painted ladies and west coast ladies. At Oakwood Valley, brown and yellow mourning cloaks and California sisters can be seen on mild mornings among the willows, and buff-colored California hairstreaks around the oaks. The endangered Mission blues found at the Headlands favor silvery lupine, although they will also lay eggs on one or two other kinds of lupines. The Golden Gate National Recreation Area has planted these lupines at the Headlands in an effort to enhance the Mission blue habitat.

Most of the Headlands' groves and woodlands dotting the hillsides are planted trees or their descendants—predominately blue-gum eucalyptus from Australia and Monterey pines and cypresses, which grow indigenously on the California coast but not in the Headlands. They were originally planted here by dairy farmers as windbreaks and by the U.S. Army as ornamentals around buildings. You may be surprised to find under these trees, even during the rainless summers, a thick carpet of green grass where the trees intercept the frequent summer fogs, which collect in droplets on the leaves and fall like rain.

Arboreal Imperialism

Although there are scattered scrub oaks throughout the Headlands, the only true oak woodland here is in Oakwood Valley at the northeast corner of the park. Here, along the deep soil of the grassy valley bottom and far enough inland to be sheltered from the brisk, damp winds off the ocean, you enter the domain of the coast live oak. If you come from other parts of the country, you may not recognize this tree as an oak; it keeps its leaves the year around. And the leaves are not the typical lobed oak leaf, they're oval, from one to three inches long, often with spiny edges and convex on top, concave beneath. A familiar (although not infallible) identification sign is the shape: If the leaf, upside down, can hold water, it's from a coast live oak.

The live oaks (there are several varieties) were known to the Spaniards as "encinas" in distinction to the "robles," the deciduous oaks growing farther inland. The trunks of the coast live oaks in Oakwood Valley, as elsewhere, have an architectural splendor; often they grow upward for a few feet then extend horizontally, sometimes arching down again to ground level. Robert Louis Stevenson, encountering these oaks at Monterey, described their twisted forms as "woods for murderers to crawl among." A less morbid description would be that their gnarled gray bark and horizontal growth also make them woods for kids to climb among.

Along with the oaks are laurels, also known here as bay trees and in Oregon as pepperwood or myrtle. Their leaves are long and narrow like willow leaves, pale green on top and yellowish underneath. The entire leaf turns bright yellow when it is ready to fall, which on this evergreen can be at any time of year. Crush a fallen leaf to experience the pungent aromas, a sure identification. But don't breathe too deeply, the aroma will cause you to see stars and a headache will explode in your temples.

Under the creekbank trees, along Tennessee and Rodeo creeks, you will find blackberries and several varieties of ferns. You will also find, on the valley floor, occasional foundations of old farm buildings and some planted trees and their descendants, a few fruit trees, pines and cypresses but mostly eucalyptus of every size and shape. In some places the "eucs" form dense thickets and crowd out native vegetation;

Coast live oak

Don't just walk past a branching tree in the
Headlands without scanning the branches. If you're
lucky, you might glimpse one of those elusive ghosts
of the twilight, a great horned owl. Along the banks
of creeks and streams, where water-loving trees like
willows and laurels set their roots, look for a splash of
yellow seep-spring monkeyflowers.

the original trees in these thickets were planted for merchantable wood early in the 20th century when the Australian trees, newly introduced to California, were reputed to be valuable for lumber. The boom did not pay off, and when the planted trees scattered their ample crop of aromatic seed pods, California was left with innumerable eucalyptus thickets nearly as impenetrable as a canebreak. The prolific trees are rampant destroyers of native vegetation, which cannot grow beneath them. In Oakwood Valley as elsewhere, there are impressive individual specimens with four-foot-thick trunks and heights of 100 feet or more, but unfortunately, they shade the native live oaks, which require abundant sunlight. National Park Service policy is to preserve indigenous trees and plants by removing the invaders.

Like other watercourses here, Oakwood Creek, which drains into San Francisco Bay, is lined in many places with willow thickets and tangles of bracken, swordferns and other matted vegetation. The slopes on the west side of the valley, partly shaded from the warm afternoon sun and consequently more moist, are thickly covered with laurel and scrub oaks. On the drier eastern slopes are occasional red-barked madrone trees, California holly (toyon) bushes with bright red berries in the fall, and the ubiquitous coyote brush, with small bright-green leaves and a cottony efflorescence in the fall responsible for its colloquial name, "fuzzy wuzzy."

The Haunting Hoot

In all of the Headlands' riparian woodlands, animals that come to drink most often under the cover of darkness are black-tailed deer, bobcats, gray foxes, and raccoons, which usually wash their food in the creek before eating it. Whether this habit is a sign of intelligence or blind instinct is questionable: Sometimes if the creek is dry the animals simply wash their food in the dust.

Swordfern

ALTHOUGH BIRDS OF MANY SPECIES inhabit the groves along the creeks, the most conspicuous bird call may be the haunting hoot of the great horned owl, heard at night and in the crepuscular hours after sunset and before sunrise. This bird is a fierce predator, able to devour not only mice, gophers, and rabbits but other birds, including small hawks. Its call may strike fear into the hearts of smaller animals, but its connotations for humans have historically been quite different. The owl has been a symbol of benevolent human wisdom since long before the ancient Greeks designated the owl of Athena as the sacred bird of the goddess. In imagination, we may hear in its "Who, who?" the questioning spirit of the forest, challenging us to define our own identity, particularly our relation to these woodlands and their community of plants and animals.

The Army at the Headlands

Visitors to San Francisco, gazing across the water at the north shore of the Golden Gate and open hills which appear very much as nature made them, may wonder how this open space could continue to exist in the midst of a Bay Area metropolis of six million people. The answer lies with the United States Army.

The Headlands are not quite as vacant as they may seem. Some of the hills and hummocks that visitors to the park may assume are natural features of the landscape are part of a system of fortifications that were operated in wartime by thousands of men in uniform. And they are but the tip of a large and complex system of underground weapons chambers, living quarters, ammunition storage magazines and command-and-control stations, some connected with honeycombs of tunnels and passageways. Many of them are now open to the public on guided tours.

The military history of the Headlands is the story of several generations of defense technology rapidly becoming obsolete with the swift development of increasingly sophisticated weapons systems. You can still see "earthwork" batteries bulwarked with dirt at Point Cavallo, dating from the 1870s. Twenty-five-ton cannons with a range of three miles were to be mounted here, able to hit any ship sailing through the Golden Gate. By the 1890s, weapons technology made these early fortifications obsolete, and the Army began to build elaborate bunkers of concrete and steel capable of housing huge rifles that could fire a half-ton shell for eight miles. But by the 1920s even these formidable weapons were made obsolete by the development of long-range battleship guns and warplanes. So the next generation of artillery included anti-aircraft weapons and 16-inch guns (as measured by the muzzle diameter) able to send one-ton projectiles 25 miles. Each emplacement was protected by a concrete enclosure with a thick overhead cover or "casemate."

By the time of World War II the entire area along the ocean and the Golden Gate was bristling with gun emplacements, anti-aircraft batteries, machine gun nests, radar installations, searchlight batteries, and lookout stations, all camouflaged to appear to be part of the natural landscape. Fortunately, the guns never faced a real enemy, but they fired at targets on or over the ocean. The thunder of the guns frequently rattled windows ten miles away in San Francisco and occasionally cracked glass or plaster.

In the aftermath of World War II, with the advent of nuclear weapons and guided missiles, even the biggest artillery became obsolete, so the big guns were dismantled and sold for scrap—some of them to the Gillette Company for conversion to razor blades. By 1954, new emplacements were built for the next generation of weapons—NIKE missiles. On guided tours of the military installations you can go underground to inspect a NIKE missile and observe the intricate steering assembly that enabled the missile to zero in on a moving target, such as an attack bomber, at a maximum distance of 90 miles. You can also see the shrapnel warhead that would explode into hundreds of lethal fragments on impact, the fuel chambers, and even a compartment capable of carrying a nuclear bomb. As the guide pushes an alarm button for a demonstration alert, *one of the large missiles is rolled into place and lifted on an elevator through a trap-door in the steel roof to firing position on the surface—all in less than one minute.*

The visitor who has been observing the Headlands as a living exhibit of the evolution of life may be sobered by the thought that the incredibly complicated NIKE weapons system can be seen as a climax of the 200 million years of evolution manifest here, beginning with the fossil radiolarians. Fortunately, however, the NIKE is a symbol not only of sophisticated systems of killing but of some momentous events that could turn the human enterprise into more hopeful channels.

In a swords-into-plowshares project, the NIKE was the first American weapon to be publicly dismantled in the Strategic Arms Limitations Treaty between the super-powers to slow the nuclear arms race. The Soviet Union simultaneously began the disassembly of its similar weapons, and this old military base had become a park where humans could rediscover their roots in nature— all portending, perhaps, a new direction in the course of the evolutionary process whose signs are so clearly visible in the cliffs and beaches, the lagoons and ponds, the woodlands and hillsides of the Marin Headlands.

The crisp white barracks of Fort Cronkhite stand sentinel near the beach in Rodeo Valley. Just across the lagoon, the former NIKE missile complex is now open for inspection by visitors.

§

Hillsides and Grasslands

THE HILLSIDES OF THE MARIN HEADLANDS offer an environment at the far end of the aesthetic spectrum from the lush woodlands, the lagoons, and the sea-carved escarpments with crashing surf. In the uplands, the mood is not intense but mellow. The colors are muted for most of the year, subtle pastels in pale brown and gray-green. The dominant motif is austere.

But look closely at the right times and you will find that these slopes are well populated. Black-tail deer appear on the hillsides or ridgelines in late afternoon and early morning; sparrows twitter in the underbrush; bobcats may appear unexpectedly in a meadow in pursuit of gophers or small rabbits. Rarely, very rarely, you may spot at a distance that elusive monarch of these hills—a mountain lion, also called cougar or puma—moving quietly through the grass or brush, long tail waving slowly.

There are two exceptions to the prevailing mood of austerity in these open hills. One is the experience of climbing to a ridgetop on a clear day and suddenly seeing a breathtaking land-and-water panorama spread before you: San Francisco Bay and the cities on its far shores, or, westward, a glitter of sun on the blue-green surface of the Gulf of the Farallones, with the islands themselves on the far horizon. In summer you may look down on a glowing white sea of fog moving in from the ocean in a slow silent flood through the canyons and valleys below.

The other exception to the austerity of the hillsides comes in the spring, when wildflowers fleck the slopes with color.

Coyotes and Monkeys

Most of these hillsides are covered with an assemblage of plants known by an unglamorous name that belies their quiet beauty and proliferation of life: coastal scrub. The most conspicuous plant of the coastal scrub is coyote brush. The folklore origin of the popular name was based on the legend that coyotes brush against the plants and leave pieces of their fur on the leaves. Actually the whitish "blossoms" that appear in the fall are not coyote fur but a cottony substance that

Alien grasses carpet the hillsides of the Headlands, including rattlesnake grass, foxtail and harding grass.

carries seeds for dispersal on the wind. The inconspicuous yellow flowers appear earlier in the summer. The small round leaves are darker than most of the other coastal scrub, and the plants are three or four feet high. They tower above the lower vegetation and act as the scrubland's principal "tree," providing food and cover for such shade-loving plants as climbing cucumber and yerba buena—the "good herb" that gave San Francisco its original name (which still designates the island anchoring the Bay Bridge). Yerba buena is a vine with small round leaves that have a mint-like aroma, and were used by the Spaniards for tea.

Also sheltered by the coyote brush you may find a badly named plant, the sticky monkey flower. While the leaves are sticky, long and narrow, it takes a fertile imagination to see in its blossoms a grinning monkey. Once established under the shelter of the coyote brush, the monkey flower may grow even higher—up to six feet. Flowers range from yellow to red and are very abundant in spring and summer. A relative, the common monkey flower, has yellow blossoms and prefers damp places around streams.

Hawk Hill

To see one of the most remarkable avian sights in the western United States, go on a clear fall day up Conzelman Road along the first ridge north of the Golden Gate to the old artillery emplacements where the road becomes one-way west and climb the trail to the ridgetop above.

This is Hawk Hill, the biggest hawk lookout in western North America. You'll see the aerial parade of hawks and other migratory birds, usually several per minute, coming from the north, then soaring in ascending spirals until they are almost out of sight. Some 200 volunteers come here regularly under the auspices of the Golden Gate Raptor Observatory to count the avian migrants. A record count for a season was reached in 1992, with total sightings of more than 20,000 birds, including 21 species of hawks.

Poisons and Sock-Snaggers

The most infamous inhabitant of the coastal scrub is poison oak, which is actually not an oak but is plenty poisonous. Watch for its shiny, bright-green leaves, which grow in threes. In the fall, the leaves turn a rusty brown or bright red, causing the unwary to pick them up for their autumn leaves collections. Even in the winter, without its leaves, the plant exudes an oil that causes the too-well-known itchy skin rash. Although some people are not susceptible to the poison, most are and give the plant a wide berth. However, the Coast Miwoks were immune to the oil and used the twigs for basket weaving and the juices to dye the baskets black.

New-growth poison oak

Also prominent in the coastal scrub are two kinds of sage: black sage *(Salvia)*, primarily a Southern California plant that reaches its northernmost range here, and sage brush *(Artemisia)*, which smells good but has toxic qualities that make it unsuitable for tea or seasoning. You should also be on the watch for poison hemlock, which is not poisonous to the touch but is deadly if swallowed by animals or humans. It is tall (up to eight feet) and often grows along roadsides and other disturbed areas. Lacy, carrot-like leaves and clusters of white flowers at the top of the stem mark this distinctive plant of European origins. Poison hemlock is said to be the plant ingested by Socrates at his execution, and a key to identification is a series of purple splotches on the stems, "the blood of Socrates."

Poison hemlock bears some resemblance to another import, fennel, a harmless plant that also grows tall along roadsides. Fennel's characteristic odor of licorice, feathery leaves, and umbrella-shaped clusters of blossoms at the tops of the stems—not white like hemlock but yellow—set it apart from the other. But when in doubt, avoid both.

Interspersed with the pastel-shaded coastal scrub on these hills are the grasslands or coastal prairie—bright green after winter rains, tawny to pale gold in summer and early fall. Most of the grasses you will see are not native but were introduced on the early cattle ranches either by plan or accident, and have largely taken over from the native bunch grasses. Perhaps the best (or worst) known of the grasses is the foxtail, which grows about 18 inches high and has purplish, hairy, seed-bearing tufts that have an affinity for animals' fur and hikers' socks. Wild barley, slightly taller, resembles the foxtail but the tufts are yellow-white. Wild oats grow taller yet, up to three feet or more, and have bristly, reddish-brown seeds that can be made into oatmeal. One native grass that has managed in limited areas to survive the invasion of European grasses is the California oat grass. It resembles the introduced wild oat but unlike the non-native grasses, which are mostly seasonal, this is a perennial and grows to three feet in height.

Sky Traffic

The birds you are most likely to see in the coastal scrub and grasslands include wrentits, towhees and white-crowned sparrows skittering in the underbrush. Their camouflage-brown color makes them hard to see, and you are more likely to hear a wrentit, for example, than to see it; its call—a series of slow chirps rapidly speeding up—resembles the slow-to-fast rhythm of a bouncing marble.

Soaring over the hills and grasslands are those giant birds, the turkey vultures (sometimes incorrectly called buzzards). You can identify them by their color—mostly black with lighter-colored trailing edges on their wings—their six-foot wingspread, and their habit of circling and dipping slowly to take advantage of every current of air, with their wings held in a shallow "V" shape. Since they feed principally on mammal carcasses and not on live prey, they can afford to take their time. Unlike most birds, vultures have a keen sense of smell and are able to scent rotting carrion. Capitalizing on this ability, utility companies have found that they can use turkey vultures to spot leaks in gas lines.

YOU MAY ALSO SEE HAWKS which are less numerous here than turkey vultures, are somewhat smaller, and soar on horizontal wings. They dive swiftly when they spot their live prey, usually rodents or rabbits, sometimes lizards, snakes, or small birds. Among the most common hawks are the red-tails. Unfortunately for identification purposes, their tails are reddish only on top, but you can glimpse the color when the birds dip or dive. If you see a smaller hawk hovering in one place, beating its wings rapidly, it's likely to be an American kestrel looking for a meal below. Only rarely here will you encounter the huge golden eagle, which has a seven-foot wingspread, with wings slightly turned up at the tips. Actually, the bird is not golden but dark brown, except for a gold patch on the back of the neck.

Coyote brush forms an oasis for birds in the scrubby hillsides of the Headlands. Juncos, sparrows and quail, to name just a few, seek shelter or a handy perch in these tangled thickets.

The Coast Miwoks

For countless seasons lost in time, the Coast Miwoks came to the Marin Headlands to hunt and harvest the grasslands and the ocean shore. A strong, muscular people, they came through Tennessee Valley or on trails now forgotten from the village of Liwanelowa near the present site of Sausalito.

In Rodeo Valley, there is a large midden marking the place where the Coast Miwoks came together year after year to roast the mussels and other shellfish they gathered nearby. After the feasting, perhaps someone very wise would tell the story of how the people were created:

"At one time the Earth was covered with water. Coyote told Frog he had decided to make some people and some food for people to eat. Frog dove under the water and brought up some sand. Coyote used the sand to make land upon which he planted pine nuts, acorns, and other food. Coyote wanted to make good people for the world, people who could gather food and use the bow and arrow. This is why he made the people with hands and feet like those of Lizard."

Mammals

Your best chance of seeing the mammals on the hillsides and the grasslands is in the dimly lit hours of morning and evening. Largest and most conspicuous are the black-tailed deer (similar to the mule deer of the Sierra Nevada but somewhat smaller), visible browsing on the scrub plants after sundown and before sunrise. Bobcats, at least twice the size of house cats, can also be seen in the magical hours of low light but are sometimes spotted during the day in Tennessee Valley and on the Bobcat Trail. They hunt birds and small mammals—gophers, rabbits, squirrels and sometimes even a small or ailing deer. The tail from which the cat takes its name is not always "bobbed." Bobcats with 14-inch long tails have led some visitors into believing they have seen a lion. Unlike the lion's tail, however, the bobcat's is white-tipped, and its light-brown coat is spotted like a leopard's.

Few people have ever seen a mountain lion in the Headlands, and in those cases it was usually an animal visiting from other areas. The animal's normal range is 100 square miles, which far outdistances the 15 square miles of the Headlands. Normally the lion is shy of humans and keeps its own distance. Among the other mammals you might see here are raccoons, gray fox, long-tailed weasels, and skunks, although they are mostly nocturnal and seldom visible in the daytime.

Bobcat

Evolving Life

In the plant and animal life on these hills, as in the rocks, plants, and animals elsewhere in the Headlands, you can find evidence of a long evolutionary process. Some of the species visible here reached their present form relatively early in the course of evolution; others are later arrivals on the scene.

Among the oldest plant species you can see here is the horsetail, which ironically bears little resemblance to any part of a horse but have bright-green, needle-like leaves. Look for it in damp areas around springs and streams. Like some of the mosses, algae and other primitive plants, horsetail dates back some 300 million to 400 million years to the time when the first animal life appeared on land and the Earth's largest coal beds were formed. Somewhat later, ferns began to evolve, represented on these hillsides mainly by the bracken. Still later, in the Age of Reptiles, cone-bearing trees developed, like the introduced Monterey pines and Monterey cypresses that grow here, native to the California coast but not to the Headlands.

Then, when the Age of Reptiles came to an end (perhaps as the result of a colossal meteor hitting the Earth), the course of evolution took a decisive turn: Plants began to develop a new way of reproducing themselves. Horsetails, ferns, and conifers all grow from single-celled spores, a non-sexual form of reproduction. (Look on the backs of some of the fern leaves to see the spores, ready for distribution by the wind.)

During that crucial interval of time, beginning about 65 million years ago, the first flowering plants appeared. Their sexual form of reproduction opened the way for the vast diversity of plants we see today—and the animals that depend on them. The colorful blossoms attracted insects, which co-evolved with the flowering plants and with the ancestors of some of the mammals visible here. Only "recently"—within the last two million years—have there been humans to enjoy the spectacle of the flowers whose descendants you can see in the Headlands each spring, sprinkling the hills and grasslands with color.

The Shape of Things to Come

We can only speculate about the future of the Marin Headlands —but with a knowledge of the past as background, we can make some informed guesses about what may happen. The ancient conflict between the ocean and the continent will continue. The roaring waves of winter will further batter these cliffs, cutting them back, creating landslides of the kind that occur each year, eroding away the edge of the land.

If human activities, particularly the burning of fossil fuels, cause the global climate to become warmer, even by a few degrees, melting of the land-based polar ice sheets could cause sea level to rise steadily, accelerating the retreat of the shoreline. Rodeo and Tennessee lagoons, now brackish-to-fresh water, would again become salty, embayments of the ocean extending for miles back into the two valleys. With a sea-level rise of 200 feet (sea-level rise after the last Ice Age was about 400 feet) Tennessee "bay" would overflow into San Francisco Bay, turning the valley into a mini-Golden Gate, growing steadily larger as the swift tidal flow between the ocean and the Bay eroded its shores.

Plants and animals would slowly adapt to the new regime, as freshwater species in the two drowned valleys were replaced by those accustomed to oceanic salinity. There would be fewer members of each species corresponding to the diminished land area. In this scenario, over several hundred thousand years or more, the Headlands could be entirely eroded away, leaving open ocean where these hills now stand, and the surf would batter the East Bay shore.

But anyone concerned about the disappearance of the Headlands can be reassured that this scenario is unlikely. The subterranean pressures resulting from the collision of tectonic plates continue to force the edge of the continent upward, and the young Coast Ranges are likely to keep growing. The attacks of the ocean along this coastline may be countered by the rise of the land—or more than countered, as has happened in the past when terraces cut by the waves at sea level were lifted high above the ocean and now in many places along the California Coast form a shelf for State Highway 1 and coastal communities. There are no such marine terraces visible within the Headlands, but there is an excellent example at Bolinas Mesa, a few miles to the north.

Marincello
Picture Gerbode Valley as the site of a city of some 30,000 people, with 50 high-rise buildings, industry, shopping centers, and a summit luxury hotel on the highest point in the Headlands.

It almost happened. In 1964, developer Thomas Frouge, in partnership with Gulf Oil, the owner of the land, unveiled his plan for a city he called Marincello. Construction of roads began, but lawsuits stopped further building. Frouge died in 1969. The Nature Conservancy bought the land from Gulf Oil and in 1972, conveyed it to the National Park Service to become part of the new Golden Gate National Recreation Area.

Spring Flowers

Paintbrush

Spring comes early to the Headlands. In January, the first pale pink flowers of miner's lettuce spring up in damp places. But the real show begins in February with the appropriately named footsteps of spring—yellow, button-like blossoms close to the ground, dainty white milk maids, sapphire-blue hounds tongue, and the rare magenta rock cress. You'll also see pink-and-white wild radish, pale-yellow to deep-blue Douglas iris, and pink

Douglas iris

shooting star, yellow buttercups, red paintbrush, and orange-gold California poppy, the official state flower. Poppies are especially abundant in March, along with the yellow flowers of goldfields, the cream to dark-yellow Franciscan wallflower (rare but found on steep cliffs near Point Bonita and Battery Spencer), and the dark purple of blue-eyed grass. Often growing in tandem with the California poppy is the blue lupine.

Poppies and lupine

In April, sky lupine reaches its peak, mantling the green hills with sheets of blue. The low-growing ground iris comes on strong, along with the yellow sunflower-like blossoms of the narrow-leaf mule ears, the red-purple flowers of common vetch, and white to purple ceanothus, more familiarly known as wild lilac.

In May the most conspicuous flower is the blue-to-purple blossom of the harvest brodiaea. In June comes the aromatic pale-pink of the penny-royal, a fragrant member of the mint family.

The most dramatic aspect of late spring and early summer are the bursts of colors among the coastal scrub

Harvest brodiaea

bushes. Sticky monkey flowers' orange-yellow competes with vivid yellow lizard tail, and sprinkled everywhere are white yarrow and pearly everlasting.

The Habitat Restoration Team

Long before it became part of the National Park system, the Headlands had been invaded by foreign plants, beginning with the European grasses introduced here by the 19th-century Spaniards. One of the most aggressive invaders is the voracious South African Capeweed, which chokes out natives, including poppies, lupine and buttercups.

On any weekend, you'll find the volunteers of the Habitat Restoration Team (a joint project of the National Park Service and the Golden Gate National Park Association) uprooting the capeweed, as well as French broom, pampas grass and other invaders.

Conceivably the Headlands could actually expand into the ocean, particularly if global warming is replaced by global cooling. New ice sheets would absorb much of the Earth's water and cause sea level to subside, as it did during the last Ice Age, exposing the sea floor for 20 miles westward.

The shorter-term future is perhaps of greater interest. If California's population continues to increase, there is a danger that growing crowds of visitors could trample the hillsides and grassland, denuding them of plants and animals, particularly if the visitors were careless and had little understanding of the natural scene. Visitor education needs to keep pace with visitor attendance if the Headlands are to retain and expand their natural regime. The National Park Service will have a mammoth job to do.

WE CAN EXPECT THAT EXOTIC species such as the brooms and thistles and European grasses will be replaced by indigenous species under the Habitat Restoration Project, the eucalyptus, pines and cypresses may be removed, and the Headlands will come to resemble more closely the appearance of this terrain when Europeans first arrived. Perhaps the most auspicious aspect of the Headlands' future will not so much be changes in the landscape as changes in the outlook of visitors who come here. The encounter with "wild" nature so close to a densely populated urban area—and the views into time afforded by this extraordinary place—may broaden the visitors' perspective beyond the merely human scale. It may open their eyes to the dominant discovery of the late 20th century—the discovery that humans are members of the larger community of nature and can only insure their own survival and fulfillment by organizing their activities to match the needs and rhythms of that community—and by developing an intimate personal relationship with the land around them and its rich diversity of life.

Marin Headlands is open every day. For more information about the Headlands, call the Visitor Center at (415) 331-1540.

What to see:
The Headlands have something for everyone: trails to hike, birds to watch, places to camp, roads to bike, beaches and seacoast fortifications to explore and a thousand spots from which to survey GGNRA's scenic riches.

Visitor Center
The Marin Headlands Visitor Center in the Fort Barry Chapel greets visitors with information about hiking and camping, interpretive walks, natural history exhibits and a bookstore.

Scenic Conzelman Road and Hawk Hill
Visitors can drive cliff-hugging Conzelman Road from the Golden Gate to Point Bonita — all the way along the Bay's narrow entrance channel. This five-mile road climbs high above the bridge towers, offering an astounding bird's-eye view of San Francisco. Vista points along Conzelman road: Battery Spencer at the crest of the first hill; several road turnouts; and Hawk Hill (Hill 129), 1.8 miles from the Golden Gate Bridge. At the spot where the road narrows to one lane and plunges headfirst down the coastline, visitors can park and walk up the concrete fire road to the top of Hawk Hill.

Rodeo Valley
Running east to west, Rodeo Valley is a long, low dip in the heart of the Marin Headlands. The valley opens into a lagoon and beach at the seashore. Two military forts once guarded Rodeo Valley's smooth hills and quiet shores. Fort Barry and Fort Cronkhite, whose structures now serve as park facilities, were nerve centers of Marin Headlands military activities long ago. Rodeo Valley is still a focal point of the Marin Headlands, where visitors can park, and walk to the beach, the backcountry, a lighthouse, the visitor center and coastal bluffs.

Kirby Cove
Kirby Cove nestles at the foot of Marin Headlands just west of the Golden Gate Bridge. The mile-long trail to Kirby Cove descends 300 feet through a grove of cypress, eucalyptus, and pine. At the cove, visitors will find a pristine wedge of beach, group camping facilities complete with tent pads, and a fabulous view of the Golden Gate Bridge from below.

East Fort Baker
East Fort Baker is an old Army post in a picturesque bayshore cove east of the Golden Gate Bridge. Apart from a popular fishing pier, East Fort Baker's public amenities include a number of grassy areas and coastal bluffs for picnicking. Nearby, the Lime Point Light and foghorn sit under the bridge in the flat spot once slated for Fort Point's counterpart in Marin.

Tennessee Valley
Tennessee Valley meanders for two miles through serene, rolling hills down to a tiny cove. Out under the surf, off the cove's black beach, lies the shipwreck of the *S.S. Tennessee,* the namesake of this valley. The valley's wide, well-groomed trail offers an easy walk, bike, or horseback ride to the ocean.

Gerbode Valley and the backcountry
Just inside the coastal zone of the Marin Headlands lies GGNRA's wilderness backcountry—a hiker's paradise. An extensive network of trails traverse this landscape of grassland and coastal chaparral. Every hilltop is a panaromic vista point; every valley is a chance to smell fennel and sage, or catch a fleeting glimpse of a bobcat or bush rabbit.

California quail

Birdwatching

Rodeo Lagoon and Bird Island are favorite birdwatching spots in the Rodeo Valley area. Just offshore, Bird Island's guano-white crags throng with cormorants, gulls, and brown pelicans. Inland, visitors can see egrets, ducks, and other birds feeding and resting in the shallow wetlands of Rodeo Lagoon.

Walking and hiking

Rangers lead a variety of special walks through the Marin Headlands every month with themes ranging from birding and wildflowers to coastal batteries. Call (415) 331-1540 for current schedule. For more details, pick up the Marin Headlands Trail Guide at the Visitor Center.

Biking

Many old fire and ranch roads in the Headlands are good for mountain biking. The Tennessee Valley trail offers a leisurely bike ride to the beach. Please give way to hikers, horses, and walkers sharing the trail. Biking is prohibited on footpaths and open terrain. Check at the Visitor Center for current regulations.

Horseback riding

Tennessee Valley's Miwok stables provide interpretive guided horseback rides to Muir Beach and other areas. Call (415) 383-8048 for information.

Camping

Please reserve campgrounds well in advance (maximum 90 days). For permits and reservations, call (415) 331-1540.

For your safety

Take water on hiking trips.
Beware of poison oak and ticks.
Watch out for dangerous waves at the seashore. Never turn your back on the sea.
Cliffs are hazardous and unsuitable for climbing.

What to wear

Be prepared for weather fluctuating between sunshine and fog, particularly in the summer.

Suggested Reading

DeCoster, Miles, Mark Klett, Mike Mandel, Paul Metcalf and Larry Sultan. *Headlands: The Marin Coast at the Golden Gate.* University of New Mexico Press, 1989.

Evans, Jules C. *The Natural History of Point Reyes.* Point Reyes National Seashore Association, 1988.

Garth, John S. and Tilden, J.W. *California Butterflies.* University of California Press, 1986.

Gilliam, Harold. *Weather of the San Francisco Bay Region.* University of California Press, 1962.

Howell, John Thomas. *Marin Flora.* Second Edition. University of California Press, 1970.

Jameson, E.W., Jr. and Peeters, Hans, Jr. *California Mammals.* University of California Press, 1988.

Shanks, Ralph and Shanks, Lisa Woo, Editor. *Guardians of the Golden Gate: Lighthouses and Lifeboat Stations of San Francisco Bay.* Costano Books, 1990.

Teather, Louise. *Place Names of Marin.* Scottwall Associates, 1986.

Wahrhaftig, Clyde, and Murchie, Benita. *Marin Headlands, California.* Geological Society of America, 1987.

About the Authors
Harold Gilliam is an environmental writer for the *San Francisco Chronicle* and has written 14 books on environmental subjects. His wife, Ann Lawrence Gilliam, has collaborated with him as editor or co-author on several books and is co-author of their most recent book, *Creating Carmel: The Enduring Vision.*

Acknowledgments
In addition to people mentioned in the text of this book, we would like to extend special thanks to Dr. Clyde Wahrhaftig of the United States Geological Survey and the University of California for extensive assistance with the chapter on Headlands geology; to editor Nora Deans for shaping our manuscript into this book; and to the very devoted staff and volunteers who provided us with on-the-spot information during our explorations of the Headlands.

The Golden Gate National Park Association wishes to thank the staff of the Golden Gate National Recreation Area who helped review and produce this publication.

GGNPA PRODUCTION MANAGEMENT
CHARLES MONEY
GREG MOORE

EDITOR
NORA L. DEANS

DESIGN
NANCY E. KOC

PHOTOGRAPHY
ALL PHOTOGRAPHS BY BRENDA THARP EXCEPT:

GGNRA ARCHIVES (PAGES 13, 30, 38-39, 44)

ILLUSTRATIONS
ANN CAUDLE, © 1993 MONTEREY BAY AQUARIUM (PAGE 11)
KAREN MONTGOMERY (PAGE 4)
LAWRENCE ORMSBY (PAGES 1, 2, 17, 19, 22, 23, 24, 32, 36, 46, 47, 48)
DAVID RICKMAN (PAGE 27)
TODD TELANDER (PAGES 18, 20, 25, 33, 34, 53)

SET IN SABON ANTIQUA

PRINTED IN HONG KONG ON RECYCLED PAPER